A children's guide to birdwatching

BIRD SPOTTER'S GUIDE

Identify over 100 birds

nosy crow

First published in the United Kingdom in 2016 by Nosy Crow Ltd
The Crow's Nest, 10a Lant Street
London SE1 1QR
www.nosycrow.com

ISBN 978 0 85763 580 8

The words 'The National Trust' and the oak leaf logo are registered trademarks of the National Trust for England, Wales and Northern Ireland used under licence from National Trust (Enterprises) Limited (Registered Company Number 01083105)

Nosy Crow and associated logos are trademarks and/or registered trademarks of Nosy Crow Ltd (Registered Company Number 7130282)

Text © Robyn Swift 2016
Illustrations © Mike Langman 2016

The right of Robyn Swift to be identified as the author and Mike Langman to be identified as the illustrator of this work has been asserted.

A CIP catalogue record for this book is available from the British Library.

Printed in China by Imago
Papers used by Nosy Crow are made from wood grown in sustainable forests.

1 3 5 7 9 8 6 4 2

Picture references
Cover (t) Menno Schaefer/Shutterstock.com
(b) Samuel Borges Photography/Shutterstock.com (b) djgis/Shutterstock.com
P4 © Steve Horsley/Shutterstock.com P6 © Alpha C/Shutterstock.com
P7 © Targn Pleiades/Shutterstock.com P9 (t) © Juha-Pekka Kervinen/Shutterstock.com
P9 (m) © vivanm/Shutterstock.com P9 (b) © Kuttelvaserova Stuchelova/Shutterstock.com
P11 (t) © gabrisigno/Shutterstock.com P11 (b) © Vishnevskiy Vasily/Shutterstock.com
P12 © jps/Shutterstock.com P13 (t) © Maria Gaellman/Shutterstock.com
P13 (b) © S.Cooper Digital/Shutterstock.com P15 (t) © Rob kemp/Shutterstock.com
P15 (b) © David Dohnal/Shutterstock.com P16 (t) © Kletr/Shutterstock.com
P16 (b) © Adam Fichna/Shutterstock.com P17 (t) © Danny Alvarez/Shutterstock.com
P17 (b) © AndreAnita/Shutterstock.com P18 © Abi Warner/Shutterstock.com
P19 (t) © Adam Fichna/Shutterstock.com P19 (b) © Gertjan Hooijer/Shutterstock.com
P20 © kzww/Shutterstock.com P24 © Nadiia Korol/Shutterstock.com
P25 & 26 © Erni/Shutterstock.com P27 © PetrP/Shutterstock.com

CONTENTS

INTRODUCTION

Birdlife is amazing! There are so many different species – nearly 10,000! And you don't need to go far to see them because birds live everywhere, from seashores and mountains to gardens and city streets. If you look out of a window for long enough, you're sure to see or hear a bird – whether you're in the country, or even in a busy town. All you need to become a birdwatcher are your eyes, your ears and a little bit of patience.

Look out for robins in the snow.

This book is split into two parts to help anyone who's a complete beginner at birdwatching. The first part is an introduction to birdlife, as well as the skills you will need to enjoy watching birds.

Bullfinch (female)

The second part is a guide to some of the birds you may be able to see in Britain, packed with pictures and tips for identifying lots of different species. The guide groups families of birds together, which should make it easier to quickly identify a bird when you're out and about birdwatching – all the water birds are together, for example, followed by the birds of prey.

Dunlin (winter)

The more you look at birds, the more fascinating they become. You can watch them however and wherever you like. Just remember to have fun and you'll soon be an expert!

Pied wagtail (winter)

IDENTIFICATION

Some birds are very easy to identify, but others are a little bit trickier. It gets easier with lots of practice, and you'll soon learn what to look for so that you can tell different birds apart. If you spot a mystery bird, don't reach for your Spotter's Guide in panic, just stay still and keep your eyes firmly on it. It's important to collect as many clues about the bird as you can by asking yourself some key questions.

WHAT SIZE IS IT?

This book gives you birds' lengths in centimetres. To get this measurement, imagine the bird lying on its back and measure from the tip of the bill all the way to the tip of the tail. But that is not always helpful when you are looking at a living wild bird! Try to compare it to a bird you know and, if possible, a bird that you can see at the same time. For example, ask yourself if it is smaller than a robin.

WHAT SHAPE IS IT?

Some birds have long legs and long thin beaks; others are short and stocky. Does the bird look like any you already know? This should give you a clue as to which section of the guide the bird can be found in.

cormorant

sparrow

snipe

kingfisher

goldcrest

pigeon

WHAT COLOUR IS IT?

Look at the colour of the bird's feathers, bill and legs. Are there any striking colours or obvious features? Remember that some species have different plumage (feathers) in summer and winter, and in some species the males and females don't look alike. Also, sometimes young birds look different to adults of the same species.

Goldfinch in flight

WHAT IS IT DOING?

Pay attention to how the bird behaves. Is it out in the open or hiding in the bushes? Is it on its own or in a group? How does it feed? Does it hop, walk or run? Does it fly in a straight line or up and down? The answers to these questions should all provide you with useful clues when identifying a mystery bird.

WHAT DOES IT SOUND LIKE?

Sometimes you will hear a bird before you can see it. Or you will hear a bird, but it will fly past before you get a chance to identify it. When this happens, it's useful to be able to recognise birds by their sounds. You can hear birds using their calls to communicate with each other throughout the year, but in springtime you can hear glorious birdsong, too.

IDENTIFICATION

BILLS

If you've spotted a bird that you've never seen before, a good place to start is to look closely at its beak, or bill. You can work out what kind of food a bird eats by the shape of its bill and this will usually help you to identify which family the bird belongs to.

Waders have long, narrow bills for exploring soft mud and sandy beaches for food.

Wildfowl use their bills to 'dabble'. This is when they open their bill while skimming it across the surface of the water to trap food.

The thrush family have straight bills which are the perfect shape for eating fruit, worms and berries.

Water birds like herons, grebes and terns catch fish with their dagger-shaped bills.

Birds of prey use their hooked bills to tear strips of meat.

Finches have bills with a sharp point and strong edges for cracking open seeds and nuts.

Some bills work like tweezers, while others are more like drinking straws. As well as feeding, bills can also be used for preening and collecting materials to make nests.

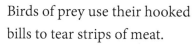

FOOTPRINTS

You have to look very closely to see birds' tracks because birds spend most of their time in the air and, when they are on the ground, they are very light on their feet. Sometimes you can see tracks in the snow, sand or mud – why don't you record them by sketching or taking a photograph before they get washed away?

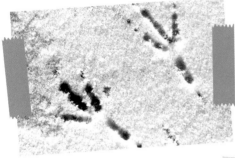

Small birds like sparrows and other songbirds have four thin toes, including one pointing backwards. They often hop, leaving pairs of footprints on the ground.

Larger birds like pigeons leave zig-zagging alternating tracks because they walk along the ground. They have one long central toe and two slightly shorter toes on either side.

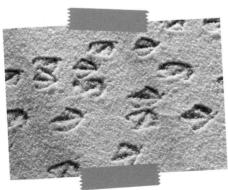

Birds that spend a lot of time swimming, like ducks, geese and swans, have webbing between their toes. Their feet act like paddles and provide extra power under the water.

9

LABELLING BIRDS

All birds have features in common – for instance, they all have wings, feathers and a bill. But when it comes to identifying birds using the field guide section, it will help to know the names of their more detailed body parts, too.

crown

forehead

nape

wing

beak or bill

back

Linnet (female)

throat

breast

flank

belly

feet

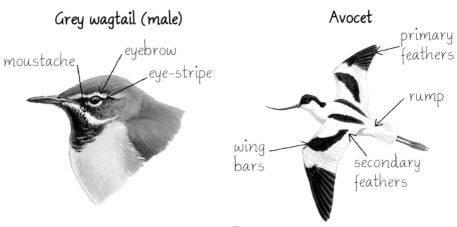

Grey wagtail (male)

moustache

eyebrow

eye-stripe

Avocet

primary feathers

rump

wing bars

secondary feathers

NESTS AND EGGS

NESTS

All birds start life in an egg in a nest. You can sometimes spot nests in the treetops or hedgerows, but remember not to get too close or take eggs that you find in the wild. The female bird lays the eggs and sits on them until the chicks are ready to hatch. Smaller birds lay smaller eggs and these take less time to hatch; bullfinches sit on their eggs for two weeks, but it takes nearly six weeks for a swan's egg to hatch!

Shag in its nest

EGGS

Fieldfare nestlings

Chicks have a tiny 'egg tooth' on the tip of their bill, which they use to break the eggshell and struggle out. Many birds are born blind and featherless. They make cheeping noises as they call for food and their parents have to fly to and from the nests to feed them. The chicks are called nestlings until they grow their flight feathers and learn to fend for themselves.

FEATHERS AND FLIGHT

FEATHERS

Birds are the only animals with feathers – and together all of a bird's feathers are called its plumage. Birds' feathers enable them to fly, and keep them warm and dry. Feathers come in different colours and patterns, which help birds to attract mates or hide from predators.

Birds stay dry even when it's raining because their outer feathers are coated with a waterproof oil, which water droplets run straight off. The plumage of some birds, like ducks, contains so much waterproof oil that they float like boats in the water! It's important for birds to take good care of their feathers, keeping them in good condition all year round.

FLIGHT

Birds use their wings and tail to help them fly and control the direction of their flight. When you look up at a bird flying, try to see if it is flapping, soaring, gliding or hovering.

Manx shearwaters glide over the water.

Chaffinches beat their wings up and down in flapping flight.

Buzzards soar in rising circles.

Kestrels can hover in the air in one spot.

HABITATS

A habitat is a bird's home, and different species choose to live in different types of habitat. When you go birdwatching, first ask yourself which birds you are likely to see in the environment you are in. This will help you to narrow down the possible birds you might spot. For example, when you are by the coast, you can expect to see gulls and terns, but not garden birds. Where there are a variety of habitats, such as forests leading to mountains, you are likely to see many different species.

GARDENS AND PARKS

The best way to start birdwatching is in your own garden or a local park. You will quickly get to know common garden birds well because you'll see the same birds time and time again. In order to attract lots of birds, there should be plenty of food, water and nesting places. This is especially important in winter because it is difficult for birds to find food on their own – the ground is frozen, insects are hiding and there is no fruit to be found on the trees.

FEED THE BIRDS

You can feed the birds in your garden with birdseed, fruit, nuts, cheese, oats or even potato! But be careful not to put out salted or roasted peanuts, milk or cooked porridge. Birds have trouble digesting these foods and porridge will stick their beaks together! If you have a bird feeder or bird table in your garden, you will get the opportunity to see birds up close and being acrobatic. As lots of birds are attracted to the food, they fly around, peck and sometimes even fight each other.

You can easily identify a nuthatch because it walks head first down the feeder.

As well as eating different foods, birds eat at different levels. While many find their food in the bushes and trees, some birds, such as swallows and swifts, only eat insects that they catch in the air! You will also spot lots of birds looking for food on the ground. Wrens, robins and pigeons are just some of the birds that try find worms, spiders and other insects on grassy lawns or underneath bushes.

Blackbirds grab worms from the soil, even when there are gardeners working nearby.

While some birds are very common in parks and gardens, there are others that you might only spot occasionally if you're lucky. For example, if your garden is near a pond or lake, you might see a heron flying over on its way to hunt for fish!

HABITATS

WOODLANDS AND FORESTS

Woodlands with lots of different types of trees, including evergreens, are the best for birdwatching. This is because the trees provide good night-time roosts (sleeping places) for birds and daytime roosts for owls. Older trees may also have plenty of holes for nesting birds.

The best times to spot birds are winter and spring, before the leaves on the trees come out and block your view. To find birds in the woods, walk slowly and stop often, listen for calls and songs, and look out for flashes of movement in the trees.

Nesting blue tits

FIELDS AND HEDGES

Many wild birds can be found on farmland, where crops and livestock attract lots of insects, which in turn means there is always plenty of food available. Look out for birds flying behind a tractor as the plough turns the soil and disturbs insects ready for them to eat. You are likely to find most birds around the edges of fields, in the hedgerows where they build their nests in spring and early summer. You will often see pheasants dashing around and whirring their wings!

Pheasant whirring its wings

LAKES AND PONDS

Lakes and ponds usually have lots of birds feeding on and under the water and around the muddy shores. You will mostly see ducks, swans and geese, which have webbed feet for swimming and bills specially designed to help them feed underwater. Some ducks, such as tufted ducks and pochards, dive to the bottom of the water to catch their food! You might also see water birds, such as grebes and herons, catching fish with their dagger-like bills.

Ducks upend to reach food underwater.

COASTS

Along the coast, you will notice a variety of different habitats, including sandy shores, pebbly beaches and rocky sea cliffs. Many birds nest on the cliffs in the spring after spending the whole winter at sea! If you're by the coast, look out for small wading birds like sanderlings or knots. They like to feed along the high-tide lines, picking food from the wet sand.

Gannets nest in colonies on rocky islands.

HABITATS

ESTUARIES

Estuaries are the wide, muddy areas where a river joins the sea. Here you can find wading birds feeding on the crabs, shellfish and worms that live in the mud. The tide changes twice a day. Just before high tide is the best time to go birdwatching, because the water is closest to the shore so the birds will be closer to you. When the water flows away from the shore at low tide, the birds will be too far in the distance for you to see. It's a good idea to check local tide times before you set out.

Ringed plover feeding in the mud

Lots of the long-legged waders look similar, so it is sometimes tricky to identify them. To give you a hint, pay attention to how the birds are eating. Some waders, like ringed plovers, peck at the surface of the mud before running to the next spot. Others, like dunlins, walk along with their long bills constantly stabbing the mud like the needle of a sewing machine.

HILLS AND MOUNTAINS

Birdwatching in the hills and mountains can be difficult, as there are very few birds to be seen. That's because the weather can be harsh, there is little shelter and there is not very much on offer for birds to eat. However, the birds that can survive here are some of the most exciting! Birds of prey, such as kestrels and buzzards, often fly over mountains and hills to hunt for small birds and animals to eat. They have such fantastic eyesight that when they are circling in the air they can spot a mouse making the slightest movement on the ground below!

You might hear a buzzard's *peeee-uuuu* call before you see it overhead.

It can sometimes be very tricky to spot birds if their feathers are camouflaged. This helps them to blend into the background – hiding from animals that they want to eat or from animals that want to eat them.

Meadow pipits are often the only small birds in the hills.

ALL YEAR ROUND

You can have fun birdwatching throughout the whole year. Many of the birds you see will have come from far away. Twice a year, birds fly thousands of miles to find food and a place to breed. This is called migration and the birds are known as migrants. Here are some suggestions for interesting things to do and see each month.

JANUARY

WHAT TO DO: Take part in the Big Garden Birdwatch by keeping a record of the birds you see in your garden and sending in your results. Ask your teacher if your class can take part in the Big Schools' Birdwatch. Find out more at www.rspb.org.uk

YOU MIGHT SEE: Flocks of yellowhammers, reed buntings, finches and larks near farmland.

FEBRUARY

WHAT TO DO: Ask an adult to help you put up a nest box. Nest boxes make perfect homes for small birds who are struggling to find a good nesting site. Make sure you get them up before the end of the month and keep them a safe distance away from cats.

YOU MIGHT SEE: Geese, ducks and waders if you visit an estuary.

MARCH

WHAT TO DO: Some early migrants, such as wheatears, begin to arrive. Keep a record of the dates when you first see a new migrant species.
YOU MIGHT SEE: Herons and rooks flying to their nests, which may already contain eggs, or even chicks!

APRIL

WHAT TO DO: Most migrant species arrive in April and May so keep recording every new visitor you see. Visit the coast to spot more migrant birds at sea crossing points.
YOU MIGHT SEE: Garden birds, like house sparrows, starlings and blackbirds, will be busy nest-building and feeding their young.

Starling (spring)

MAY

WHAT TO DO: Get up early to listen to the dawn chorus. Visit woodlands or the countryside just before daylight for the best experience!
YOU MIGHT SEE: Swifts racing over rooftops and lots of garden birds breeding. You might also see baby birds – keep your distance! Don't be tempted to rescue them as their parents are nearly always nearby.

JUNE

WHAT TO DO: Visit a colony of seabirds on the coastal cliffs. You could see lots of puffins, guillemots, razorbills, kittiwakes, fulmars or gannets – but be prepared for the noise and smell!
YOU MIGHT SEE: Male mallards starting to moult. Their feathers look scruffy and tattered until fresh new ones grow.

Puffin

JULY

WHAT TO DO: Visit a tern colony by the coast, where the adults will be busy flying to and fro feeding their young.

YOU MIGHT SEE: Large flocks of swifts flying over towns and cities, getting ready to migrate to Africa next month.

Little tern

AUGUST

WHAT TO DO: If you are near the coast, take a boat trip out to sea and you could see migrating seabirds like Manx shearwaters.

YOU MIGHT SEE: Waders, such as curlews, returning to the estuaries for the winter.

Curlew

SEPTEMBER

WHAT TO DO: Fill up a bird feeder to put in your garden. Remember, you can feed birds all year round, but they find it more difficult to find their own food throughout the winter months. For more information about how to make your own bird food and feeder, look online.

YOU MIGHT SEE: Summer visitors starting to head south, so look out for chiffchaffs and flocks of swallows and house martins.

Chiffchaff

Swallow

OCTOBER

WHAT TO DO: Clean out your nest boxes and line them with a bed of soft material ready for birds to roost in over winter.
YOU MIGHT SEE: Redwings and fieldfares in your garden as they spend the winter in the UK after breeding in Scandinavia.

Redwing

NOVEMBER

WHAT TO DO: Find out if there are any starling roosts nearby and visit at early evening. Sometimes the birds come together in huge clouds making quite a sight!
YOU MIGHT SEE: Siskins, bramblings, redwings and fieldfares. You might be really lucky and see waxwings, too. They arrive in large numbers every few years in what are known as 'waxwing winters'.

Siskin (male)

DECEMBER

WHAT TO DO: Look up at the branches of the trees that have lost their leaves – you may find nests that were used earlier in the year.
YOU MIGHT SEE: Large flocks of gulls heading to roost. Try to identify all the different species flocking together.

Black-headed gull (winter)

THE KIT

You can have fun looking for birds with no equipment at all, but if you discover that you enjoy it, then you can start building a basic birdwatching kit.

BINOCULARS

It can be difficult to see birds close up because they fly away from danger or perch high in the trees. A pair of binoculars will help you to see birds in the distance. Binoculars, or 'bins', come in different sizes and magnification powers, which affect how closely you will be able to see the bird.

Binoculars should:
* be lightweight and comfortable. You don't want to be wearing a heavy pair of binoculars all day, and you need to be able to hold them steady.
* be clear and bright when you look through them.
* focus easily.

Practise using your binoculars by using them on different things around the garden, not just birds. When you would like a closer look at a bird, keep your eyes focused on the bird and raise your binoculars up to your eyes. Don't try to look for birds through your binoculars first. Remember to keep the sun behind you because looking into bright light makes it very difficult to see any more than a silhouette and can also harm your eyes. Take good care of your binoculars by always using the neck strap, keeping the lenses clean and protecting them from bumps.

Lapwings in flight

A NOTEBOOK

A notebook is an excellent place to keep a record of birds in the wild. You can make notes about birds that you don't recognise or write down anything you don't want to forget. Note down any calls that you hear, draw simple sketches, add photographs – whatever you add is up to you! Your notebook is like a diary, so try to keep a record of the date and time for each entry and you can look back over them and notice how birdlife changes over seasons.

BIRD SPOTTER'S NOTEBOOK

A FIELD GUIDE

Probably the most important part of a birdwatcher's kit is a good field guide (like the second section of this book). A guide will help you discover what different birds look like, where and when you might see them and any interesting characteristics of the species. Most field guides show birds in a similar order, grouped by families. So, if you're by the sea, you know to look in the seabirds section of your field guide. From there you should be able to identify the species by looking at the illustrations and reading the descriptions.

BIRDWATCHING TIPS

Willow warbler

Once you're ready to get outside and start exploring birdlife, these tips should help you to become a better birdwatcher and improve your chances of seeing lots of birds.

BIRDS COME FIRST!

There are a few golden rules to follow when you go out birdwatching:
• Try not to disturb the birds you are watching – don't get too close or chase them if they start to move away.
• Don't approach birds when they're at their nest with their young, and never be tempted to pick up eggs.
• Leave baby birds alone – their parents are probably nearby.

MOVEMENT

Move gently and slowly, looking for any signs of bird movement and trying not to disturb the habitat. Stop and stand still frequently and listen carefully for bird sound. Remember to look up, down and behind you – you can find birds at any level!

CLOTHING

First, make sure you're wearing the right clothing. Birds will find it harder to spot you if you're camouflaged wearing dull colours, rather than standing out in bright clothing. Try to wear clothes that don't rustle so you don't scare birds away and you can hear them more easily, too.

If you're going to be spending time outside watching birds, make sure your clothes protect you from the weather: sun hat and suncream in the summer, or lots of layers, gloves and a hat in the winter. And don't forget wellies if you're visiting anywhere muddy!

TIME

Do your research into the best time of day to see different species and look up the tide times if you're visiting the sea. Soon after dawn is usually when birds are most active, but late afternoon and early evening are good times, too. You are less likely to see birds during the middle of the day, when it is hottest.

RESPECT THE COUNTRYSIDE

As well as not disturbing any birds, there are a few more guidelines to remember when you're out and about in the countryside:

- Respect the environment and protect habitats
– try not to damage the places where birds live.
- Be careful not to trespass on private land –
always tell an adult where you are going and
make sure you have permission.
- Always follow the Countryside Code.
- Be polite to other birdwatchers.
- Follow the bird protection laws.

More information can be found by exploring the resources listed on the next page.

Great spotted woodpecker

USEFUL INFORMATION

There are plenty of resources that can help you to take your interest in birdwatching further. Here's a list of some useful websites, books, organisations and more that will inspire you.

ORGANISATIONS

RSPB (Royal Society for the Protection of Birds): www.rspb.org.uk
Find an A to Z of birds, listen to birdsong and watch video clips. You can also take part in the annual Big Garden Birdwatch (www.rspb.org.uk/birdwatch) and you'll find lots of games and activities if you explore the RSPB Kids page (www.rspb.org.uk/youth).

Wildfowl & Wetlands Trust: www.wwt.org.uk
Find out about the wetland centres near you and maybe plan a visit.

The Wildlife Trusts (and Wildlife Watch): www.wildlifetrusts.org
Discover nature reserves across the country.

British Trust for Ornithology: www.bto.org
Here you will find information about where Britain's birds live, what they do and links to recent survey results.

ACTIVITIES

Find out how to make a nest box on the BBC website: www.bbc.co.uk/breathingplaces/nest_box/

Find out how to make a recycled bird feeder as well as lots of other bird-based activities: www.naturedetectives.org.uk

WEBSITES

BirdLife International: www.birdlife.org
This website is packed with information about the conservation of birds around the world.

BirdGuides: www.birdguides.com
Find news about birds, as well as photographs and information about all the different species you might see.

BBC Nature: www.bbc.co.uk/nature/life/Bird
Here you will find nestcam videos, identification guides and a fantastic library of bird-related information videos.

Fatbirder: www.fatbirder.com
This site is full of facts, news and information about equipment, worldwide species of birds and places to visit.

BOOKS

RSPB Children's Guide to Bird Watching, Bloomsbury, 2007

RSPB Birdwatching for Beginners, Dorling Kindersley, 2013

MAGAZINES

There are monthly magazines dedicated to birdwatching, where you can find up-to-date articles and information. Popular magazines to try are *Bird Watching* and *Birdwatch*.

Male and female mallard

FIELD GUIDE

LITTLE GREBE

summer

winter

Little grebes are small and brown with a fluffy rear end. They have a reddish neck and cheeks and a pale yellow patch at the base of the bill.

SIZE:	27 cm
WHERE TO SEE:	Ponds, lakes, canals and rivers with plenty of plant life
WHEN TO SEE:	January–December
WHAT THEY EAT:	Small fish, insects, tadpoles and molluscs
SOUNDS LIKE:	Loud, whinnying trill; silent in winter
LOOKS LIKE:	Young moorhen, coot

GREAT CRESTED GREBE

winter

Great crested grebes have an upright neck and a pointed bill. In summer, they have a shaggy ruff on their cheeks and a black, backward-facing tuft.

SIZE:	48 cm
WHERE TO SEE:	Lakes and reservoirs, sometimes the coast
WHEN TO SEE:	January–December
WHAT THEY EAT:	Mainly fish
SOUNDS LIKE:	Mostly silent, but *gruck gruck* barks in winter
LOOKS LIKE:	Young cormorant, shag

GREY HERON

Grey herons have long
legs and a long, thin neck.
Their yellowish bill is
dagger-shaped. They have
a white forehead with a
stripe of black feathers on
the back of their head.

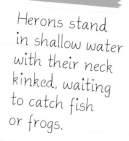

Herons stand
in shallow water
with their neck
kinked, waiting
to catch fish
or frogs.

SIZE:	92 cm
WHERE TO SEE:	Around any kind of water – ponds, lakes, rivers
WHEN TO SEE:	January–December
WHAT THEY EAT:	Fish, frogs, rats and insects
SOUNDS LIKE:	Short, harsh *kraak*; deep croak in flight
LOOKS LIKE:	Large gulls, large birds of prey

LITTLE EGRET

Little egrets are heron-shaped, but
much smaller and white all over.
Their slim bill and legs are black
and they have yellow feet.

SIZE:	60 cm
WHERE TO SEE:	Marshland and large rivers
WHEN TO SEE:	January–December
WHAT THEY EAT:	Small fish, frogs and snails
SOUNDS LIKE:	Usually silent
LOOKS LIKE:	Barn owl, gulls (in flight)

WHITE STORK

White storks are large white wading birds with black feathers on their wings. They have bright red legs and a long red bill. Storks often build their nests high on rooftops.

SIZE:	102 cm
WHERE TO SEE:	Very rare in Britain; sometimes found in open land near water
WHEN TO SEE:	April–October
WHAT THEY EAT:	Frogs, mice, insects and small fish
SOUNDS LIKE:	Silent, but clap their bill when greeting
LOOKS LIKE:	Grey heron

GANNET

Gannets are the same size as a goose. They are white all over with black wing tips, a long, pointed bill and a yellow head. When catching fish, gannets circle above the sea and dive down from heights of up to 40 metres.

SIZE:	92 cm
WHERE TO SEE:	Cliffs close to the coast
WHEN TO SEE:	January–December
WHAT THEY EAT:	Fish, such as mackerel and herring
SOUNDS LIKE:	Silent at sea, but barking *arr arr* at nest
LOOKS LIKE:	Large gulls

CORMORANT

Cormorants often stand with their wings held out open to dry.

Cormorants are large black birds with white cheeks and an orangey-yellow patch near their bill. They have a small hook at the end of their bill and their feathers have a bronze-coloured sheen.

SIZE:	92 cm
WHERE TO SEE:	Around the coast, often near harbours, but also inland lakes
WHEN TO SEE:	January–December
WHAT THEY EAT:	Fish
SOUNDS LIKE:	*Khro khro* croaks at nest
LOOKS LIKE:	Shag

SHAG

Shags are smaller than a cormorant with a thinner bill and shorter neck. Their feathers are black with a greenish gloss and they have a short crest on their forehead.

SIZE:	78 cm
WHERE TO SEE:	Rocky coastal cliffs
WHEN TO SEE:	January–December
WHAT THEY EAT:	Fish, mainly herring and sand eels
SOUNDS LIKE:	Grunting *kroack-kraik-kroack*; silent at sea
LOOKS LIKE:	Cormorant

MUTE SWAN

Mute swans are large, familiar birds with a very long neck. Adults are bright white with an orange and black bill and young swans are greyish-brown.

SIZE:	140 cm
WHERE TO SEE:	Parks and rivers
WHEN TO SEE:	January–December
WHAT THEY EAT:	Plants from shallow water or grass from fields
SOUNDS LIKE:	Mostly silent, but hissing calls when angry
LOOKS LIKE:	Bewick's swan, whooper swan

WHOOPER SWAN

Whooper swans have a yellow and black bill. Their neck is longer than that of the mute swan and they hold it upright when swimming.

SIZE:	140 cm
WHERE TO SEE:	Lakes and estuaries
WHEN TO SEE:	October–March
WHAT THEY EAT:	Leaves and stems from dry ground
SOUNDS LIKE:	Trumpeting call like an old-fashioned car horn
LOOKS LIKE:	Mute swan, Bewick's swan

BEWICK'S SWAN

Bewick's swans are like smaller versions of the whooper swan with a shorter, thicker neck and less yellow on their bill.

SIZE:	120 cm
WHERE TO SEE:	Freshwater lakes, meadows and farmland
WHEN TO SEE:	November–March
WHAT THEY EAT:	Water plants and grass, and leftover grain and potatoes
SOUNDS LIKE:	Loud *kuru* calls like an excited dog
LOOKS LIKE:	Mute swan, whooper swan

GREYLAG GOOSE

Greylag geese have silvery-grey plumage, which is neatly barred. They have large orange bills and pink legs and feet.

SIZE:	82 cm
WHERE TO SEE:	Grassy fields, coastal marshes and suburban parks
WHEN TO SEE:	January–December
WHAT THEY EAT:	Grass, roots, cereals and grain
SOUNDS LIKE:	Noisy cackling and honking; *ahng-ong-ong* call in flight
LOOKS LIKE:	Canada goose

CANADA GOOSE

Canada geese are taller than other geese and have a longer neck. Their head and neck is black with white patches on their cheeks. Their body is the same shape as a swan's, but brown with paler underparts.

SIZE:	95 cm
WHERE TO SEE:	Common in towns and parks; prefers inland waters
WHEN TO SEE:	January–December
WHAT THEY EAT:	Grass, roots, leaves and seeds
SOUNDS LIKE:	Loud trumpeting *ah-honk*
LOOKS LIKE:	Greylag goose

SHELDUCK

Shelducks have white bodies with blackish-green heads and necks. They have an orange band around their chest and black markings on their wings. Males have a knob on their bright red bill.

SIZE:	61 cm
WHERE TO SEE:	Sandy or muddy areas around the coast
WHEN TO SEE:	January–December
WHAT THEY EAT:	Small shellfish, water snails and worms
SOUNDS LIKE:	Males make a low whistling noise; females have a *gagagaga* call
LOOKS LIKE:	Shoveler, mallard

WIGEON

male   female

Male wigeons have round grey bodies with chestnut heads, yellow foreheads and white patches on their wings. Females are reddish-brown with a white belly and they are both smaller than a mallard.

SIZE:	46 cm
WHERE TO SEE:	Wetlands, around the coast, lakes, reservoirs and gravel pits
WHEN TO SEE:	October–April
WHAT THEY EAT:	Water plants, grasses and roots
SOUNDS LIKE:	Males make a high *whe-ooo*; females make a purring sound
LOOKS LIKE:	Teal, mallard, pochard

TEAL

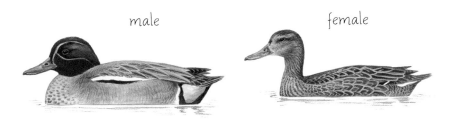

male

female

Teals are the smallest type of duck. Males have grey bodies and chestnut heads with green eyepatches and a black-edged yellow marking under the tail. Females are speckled brown and look a lot like a female mallard.

SIZE:	35 cm
WHERE TO SEE:	Mainly marshland, but also lakes and streams with lots of cover
WHEN TO SEE:	October–April
WHAT THEY EAT:	Seeds, water plants and small insects
SOUNDS LIKE:	Males make a high *crik crik*; females make a short, sharp *quack*
LOOKS LIKE:	Mallard, wigeon

MALLARD

male

female

Mallards are the most common of all the ducks. The male is grey with a green head, yellow bill, white neckband and curly black tail feathers. Females are brown and black with an orange bill.

SIZE:	58 cm
WHERE TO SEE:	Any areas of fresh water
WHEN TO SEE:	January–December
WHAT THEY EAT:	Seeds, acorns, berries, plants, insects and shellfish
SOUNDS LIKE:	Females make a *quack quack* sound; males are much quieter
LOOKS LIKE:	Shoveler, pintail, teal, wigeon

PINTAIL

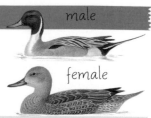
male

female

Male pintails are white and grey with a brown head and a long black tail. Females look like a female mallard, but with a pointed tail.

SIZE:	66 cm
WHERE TO SEE:	Marshland and coastal areas
WHEN TO SEE:	October–April
WHAT THEY EAT:	Mainly water plants
SOUNDS LIKE:	Mostly silent, but sometimes *quack quack*
LOOKS LIKE:	Mallard

SHOVELER

male

female

Shovelers have long, shovel-like black bills, white bodies with brown patches and dark green heads. Females are speckled brown.

SIZE:	51 cm
WHERE TO SEE:	Quiet lakes and shallow water
WHEN TO SEE:	January–December
WHAT THEY EAT:	Small insects and water plants
SOUNDS LIKE:	Males make a deep *took took*; females have a quieter *quack*
LOOKS LIKE:	Shelduck (male), mallard (female)

GADWALL

male

female

Gadwalls are smaller than a mallard and speckled grey with a black rear end. Females are speckled brown with an orange bill.

SIZE:	50 cm
WHERE TO SEE:	Quiet lakes, marsh pools and ponds
WHEN TO SEE:	January–December
WHAT THEY EAT:	Plants and seeds
SOUNDS LIKE:	Males croak in flight; females make a quacking *reck reck reck*
LOOKS LIKE:	Mallard

TUFTED DUCK

Tufted ducks have black and white plumage and golden-yellow eyes. They have a long, wispy tuft of feathers on their head and white wing bars in flight. Females are dark brown with pale flanks and a shorter crest.

male

female

SIZE:	43 cm
WHERE TO SEE:	Lakes and rivers with reeds; sometimes coastal waters
WHEN TO SEE:	January–December
WHAT THEY EAT:	Insects and plants
SOUNDS LIKE:	Mostly silent, but growling *kurr kurr* in flight
LOOKS LIKE:	Pochard

POCHARD

Male pochards are grey with an orangey-red head and neck and a black breast and tail. The females are dullish brown and grey and have a bluish ring around the bill.

male

female

Pochards sit on the water for hours, riding the waves if it is windy, or just sleeping!

SIZE:	46 cm
WHERE TO SEE:	Lakes with lots of reeds
WHEN TO SEE:	January–December
WHAT THEY EAT:	Plants and seeds, snails, small fish and insects
SOUNDS LIKE:	Mostly silent
LOOKS LIKE:	Tufted duck

PHEASANT

male   female

Male pheasants are very colourful with green heads, red faces, a copper body and a long, stiff, pointed tail. Female pheasants (called hens) are pale brown with bold black markings and a slightly shorter tail.

SIZE:	Male 87 cm; female 58 cm
WHERE TO SEE:	Farmland and the edge of woodlands
WHEN TO SEE:	January–December
WHAT THEY EAT:	Plants, seeds, berries, insects and worms
SOUNDS LIKE:	Loud, explosive *corrk-kok* call; clucking in flight
LOOKS LIKE:	Grey partridge, red grouse

RED GROUSE

Bigger than a partridge, red grouse are plump reddish-brown birds with a short tail and a small head. Their legs and feet are covered in small white feathers and the male has a red patch over the eye.

SIZE:	36 cm
WHERE TO SEE:	Moorland with no trees but lots of heather
WHEN TO SEE:	January–December
WHAT THEY EAT:	Heather, seeds, berries and insects
SOUNDS LIKE:	Loud call which sounds like *go-bak, go-bak, bak-bak-bak*
LOOKS LIKE:	Female pheasant, partridges

GREY PARTRIDGE

Grey partridges are small, hunched birds with an orange face, grey neck and breast and a dark brown mark on their lower body. Their tails look reddish in flight.

SIZE:	30 cm
WHERE TO SEE:	Open farmland with thick hedges
WHEN TO SEE:	January–December
WHAT THEY EAT:	Grass, weeds, seeds and insects
SOUNDS LIKE:	Grating *kerrick* call when excited, especially at dusk
LOOKS LIKE:	Pheasant or red-legged partridge

RED-LEGGED PARTRIDGE

Red-legged partridges are now more common than grey partridges. They have white faces bordered with black. Their bodies have striped flanks and a dark-red tail.

In autumn, red-legged partridges gather in groups (called 'coveys') which scatter when alarmed.

SIZE:	34 cm
WHERE TO SEE:	Open fields and sometimes coastal dunes
WHEN TO SEE:	January–December
WHAT THEY EAT:	Leaves, shoots, berries and acorns
SOUNDS LIKE:	Mechanical *chuck-chukka-chuck* calls or gobbling and hissing
LOOKS LIKE:	Grey partridge

RED KITE

Red kites look similar to buzzards, but you can tell them apart by the tail and wing shapes. They have a reddish-brown body, an orange forked tail and a whitish head.

SIZE:	62 cm
WHERE TO SEE:	Farmland and open countryside
WHEN TO SEE:	January–December
WHAT THEY EAT:	Dead animals (like rabbits or sheep), birds, earthworms and voles
SOUNDS LIKE:	High-pitched wailing *pee-ooo-eee*, similar to a buzzard
LOOKS LIKE:	Buzzard

BUZZARD

Buzzards are stocky with broad wings and a short, round tail. They are dark brown with a paler brown underside and their wings have dark tips.

SIZE:	54 cm
WHERE TO SEE:	Woodlands, farmland and hills
WHEN TO SEE:	January–December
WHAT THEY EAT:	Small mammals, birds and large insects
SOUNDS LIKE:	Noisy, high-pitched *peeee-uuuu*, like a cat mewing
LOOKS LIKE:	Red kite

KESTREL

male

female

Kestrels have pointed wings and a long tail. Males have a reddish-brown, spotted back and a grey head; females are brown with black markings, and both have a black band at the tip of their tail.

SIZE:	34 cm
WHERE TO SEE:	Woodlands, farmland and parks
WHEN TO SEE:	January–December
WHAT THEY EAT:	Small mammals and birds
SOUNDS LIKE:	High-pitched *ki-ki-ki-ki-ki*
LOOKS LIKE:	Hobby, sparrowhawk, cuckoo

SPARROWHAWK

Sparrowhawks have a long tail and short, broad wings. The female is larger than the male and their orange or yellow eyes give them a fierce expression.

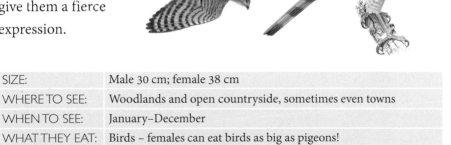

female

male

SIZE:	Male 30 cm; female 38 cm
WHERE TO SEE:	Woodlands and open countryside, sometimes even towns
WHEN TO SEE:	January–December
WHAT THEY EAT:	Birds – females can eat birds as big as pigeons!
SOUNDS LIKE:	Harsh *kek-kek-kek-kek* sound
LOOKS LIKE:	Kestrel, cuckoo

PEREGRINE

Peregrines are mostly blue-grey, with a black head and moustache marking and a white throat and cheeks. Their underside is paler and barred. They have yellow feet and yellow on the base of their bill.

Peregrines dive down on to their prey from a great height; this is called 'stooping'.

SIZE:	42 cm
WHERE TO SEE:	Hilly areas and rocky sea cliffs
WHEN TO SEE:	January–December
WHAT THEY EAT:	Medium-sized birds like pigeons and small ducks
SOUNDS LIKE:	Loud *kek-kek-kek-kek* call
LOOKS LIKE:	Kestrel, hobby, wood pigeon

HOBBY

Hobbies have long, pointed wings and a short, narrow tail. They are mainly blue-grey with streaks underneath. They have red around the legs, and a black head and moustache marking.

SIZE:	33 cm
WHERE TO SEE:	Heathland and over lakes
WHEN TO SEE:	April–October
WHAT THEY EAT:	Small birds and insects
SOUNDS LIKE:	Clear, musical *kew-kew-kew*
LOOKS LIKE:	Peregrine

Moorhens are small, plump birds. They are blackish-brown with a red and yellow bill and long green toes.

SIZE:	33 cm
WHERE TO SEE:	Lakes, ponds and rivers
WHEN TO SEE:	January–December
WHAT THEY EAT:	Water plants, seeds, insects and small fish
SOUNDS LIKE:	Loud, sudden *kruuuuuk* call
LOOKS LIKE:	Coot, little grebe

COOT

Coots are larger and rounder than moorhens with a smaller tail and red eyes. They are black all over with a white bill and forehead.

SIZE:	38 cm
WHERE TO SEE:	Lakes, ponds and reservoirs
WHEN TO SEE:	January–December
WHAT THEY EAT:	Water plants, seeds, snails and insects
SOUNDS LIKE:	Loud *kowk* call
LOOKS LIKE:	Moorhen, tufted duck, grebes

WADING BIRDS

OYSTERCATCHER

Oystercatchers have striking black and white bodies and red eyes. They have long pink legs and a long orangey-red bill.

SIZE:	43 cm
WHERE TO SEE:	Around the coast
WHEN TO SEE:	January–December
WHAT THEY EAT:	Mussels and cockles near the coast, worms inland
SOUNDS LIKE:	Loud, high-pitched *kleep-a-kleep*
LOOKS LIKE:	Avocet, lapwing

LAPWING

summer

winter

Lapwings find worms with a 'stop-run-peck' action and tap their feet on the ground to attract prey.

Lapwings have dark green backs that are glossy with purple and copper. Their underside is white and they have a short bill, steep forehead and wispy black crest.

SIZE:	30 cm
WHERE TO SEE:	Farmland and marshy areas, also along the coast
WHEN TO SEE:	January–December
WHAT THEY EAT:	Worms and insects
SOUNDS LIKE:	Loud *ee-wit* call
LOOKS LIKE:	Oystercatcher

RINGED PLOVER

If its nest is threatened, the ringed plover limps away as though injured to lead the predator away and protect its eggs.

Ringed plovers are small, plump birds with long orange legs and a black tip on their orange bill. They are sandy brown, white underneath and have a black band around their chest and face.

SIZE:	19 cm
WHERE TO SEE:	On sand and shingle beaches all around the coast
WHEN TO SEE:	January–December
WHAT THEY EAT:	Small insects and worms
SOUNDS LIKE:	Two-note whistle, *poo-eep* or *choo-wee*
LOOKS LIKE:	Sanderling

GREY PLOVER

In the winter, grey plovers are very grey, and slightly paler underneath. In the summer, they have a black face and breast. In flight, look out for their black 'armpits'.

winter

summer

SIZE:	28 cm
WHERE TO SEE:	Sandy shores and muddy estuaries
WHEN TO SEE:	January–December
WHAT THEY EAT:	Worms and shellfish from the mud
SOUNDS LIKE:	Sorrowful whistle, *pee-uu-eee*
LOOKS LIKE:	Knot, golden plover

̲DEN PLOVER

̲en plovers have a
̲all head and short
̲lack bill. They have a
gold and black patterned
back, bright white
underwings and a black
belly in summer.

summer   winter

SIZE:	28 cm
WHERE TO SEE:	Farmland and coastal marshes
WHEN TO SEE:	January–December
WHAT THEY EAT:	Worms and grubs
SOUNDS LIKE:	Two-note whistle, *pu-weee*
LOOKS LIKE:	Grey plover

AVOCET

Avocets are white with a black cap and curved black band on each side of
their back. They have long grey-blue legs and a very fine, upcurved bill.

SIZE:	43 cm
WHERE TO SEE:	Shallow coastal lagoons and muddy pools
WHEN TO SEE:	January–December
WHAT THEY EAT:	Tiny shrimps and worms
SOUNDS LIKE:	Piping *klute klute* call when alarmed
LOOKS LIKE:	Black-headed gull, oystercatcher

KNOT

In winter, knots are grey birds with a whitish belly, short grey legs and a straight black bill. In summer, their underparts are pale and coppery.

winter

SIZE:	25 cm
WHERE TO SEE:	Large muddy estuaries
WHEN TO SEE:	January–December
WHAT THEY EAT:	Insects in the summer; shellfish and worms in the winter
SOUNDS LIKE:	Quiet, dull *wutt-wutt*
LOOKS LIKE:	Redshank, dunlin, grey plover

SANDERLING

Sanderlings are mainly white birds with grey backs and dark marks on their shoulder. They have jet-black legs and a short, straight black bill.

SIZE:	20 cm
WHERE TO SEE:	Sandy beaches
WHEN TO SEE:	January–December
WHAT THEY EAT:	Worms and molluscs in the wet sand
SOUNDS LIKE:	Sharp, hard *twick twick* in flight
LOOKS LIKE:	Dunlin, knot, ringed plover

DUNLIN

Dunlins have a slightly curved bill. In winter, they are dull grey and white and in the summer they have a chestnut-coloured back.

summer

SIZE:	19 cm
WHERE TO SEE:	All around the coast; mainly wet places
WHEN TO SEE:	January–December
WHAT THEY EAT:	Insects, snails and worms
SOUNDS LIKE:	Thin, reedy *shreee* or rasping *treerrr*
LOOKS LIKE:	Knot, sanderling

TURNSTONE

summer

winter

Turnstones are a mottled chestnut-brown and black, with a bold black and white head pattern. Their underparts are white and their legs are orange.

SIZE:	23 cm
WHERE TO SEE:	Around rocky coasts; mainly shores with rock pools and seaweed
WHEN TO SEE:	January–December
WHAT THEY EAT:	Insects and molluscs
SOUNDS LIKE:	*Tuk-a-tuk-tuk* call in flight
LOOKS LIKE:	Ringed plover, oystercatcher

CURLEW

Curlews are streaked greyish-brown all over with a whiter belly, a long, downcurved bill and long grey legs.

SIZE:	55 cm
WHERE TO SEE:	Around the coast and boggy areas
WHEN TO SEE:	January–December
WHAT THEY EAT:	Worms, shellfish and insects from the mud
SOUNDS LIKE:	Very musical, rising *courlee* call
LOOKS LIKE:	Young gulls, bar-tailed godwit

BAR-TAILED GODWIT

Bar-tailed godwits are smaller than curlews and they have a slightly upturned bill.

SIZE:	37 cm
WHERE TO SEE:	All around the coast
WHEN TO SEE:	January–December
WHAT THEY EAT:	Worms, snails and insects
SOUNDS LIKE:	Quick, yelping *kiruk kiruk* call in flight
LOOKS LIKE:	Curlew, redshank, greenshank

BLACK-TAILED GODWIT

Black-tailed godwits have a straighter bill and their legs are longer above the 'knee' than the bar-tailed godwit.

SIZE:	40 cm
WHERE TO SEE:	Estuaries and wetlands
WHEN TO SEE:	January–December
WHAT THEY EAT:	Worms, snails and insects
SOUNDS LIKE:	Noisy *weeka-weeka-weeka*
LOOKS LIKE:	Oystercatcher, bar-tailed godwit

WHIMBREL

Whimbrels look like miniature curlews with dark stripes on their head, long legs and a long bill that curves near the tip.

SIZE:	40 cm
WHERE TO SEE:	Around the coast, rocky shores and moorland
WHEN TO SEE:	April–September
WHAT THEY EAT:	Insects, snails and worms
SOUNDS LIKE:	Rapid *titti-titti-titti-titti*, often repeated seven times
LOOKS LIKE:	Bar-tailed godwit, curlew

REDSHANK

Redshanks have bright orange-red legs and a medium-length bill with an orange base. They have a white rump and wing panels and a pale belly.

SIZE:	28 cm
WHERE TO SEE:	Estuaries and marshes
WHEN TO SEE:	January–December
WHAT THEY EAT:	Insects, worms and molluscs
SOUNDS LIKE:	Musical *teeu-tu-tu* call and a yodelling *lew-lew-lew*
LOOKS LIKE:	Greenshank, green sandpiper, ruff

GREENSHANK

Greenshanks have long green legs and a slightly upturned bill. They have a dark grey back and clear white underparts.

SIZE:	30 cm
WHERE TO SEE:	Around the coast, estuaries and boggy moorland
WHEN TO SEE:	January–December
WHAT THEY EAT:	Worms, snails and fish
SOUNDS LIKE:	Ringing three-part *tew-tew-tew* flight call
LOOKS LIKE:	Redshank, green sandpiper, ruff, bar-tailed godwit

GREEN SANDPIPER

Green sandpipers are smaller than redshanks with greenish legs and a grey bill. They have dark brown upperparts and a white rump in flight.

SIZE:	23 cm
WHERE TO SEE:	Muddy edges of reservoirs and freshwater lakes
WHEN TO SEE:	January–December
WHAT THEY EAT:	Insects
SOUNDS LIKE:	Loud, full-throated *tweet, weet-weet*
LOOKS LIKE:	Common sandpiper, ruff, redshank

COMMON SANDPIPER

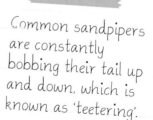

Common sandpipers are constantly bobbing their tail up and down, which is known as 'teetering'.

Common sandpipers are slightly smaller than green sandpipers and they have a more crouching posture. Their heads and upperparts are brown and they have dull yellow legs and a white belly.

SIZE:	20 cm
WHERE TO SEE:	Reservoirs, streams, muddy estuaries – all kinds of water
WHEN TO SEE:	March–October
WHAT THEY EAT:	Insects
SOUNDS LIKE:	Shrill *swee-wee-wee* flight call
LOOKS LIKE:	Green sandpiper, dunlin

RUFF

male
(spring)

juvenile

Ruffs have small heads, a short bill and orangey-red legs. They are mainly brownish-grey, but during springtime males have a colourful ruff of feathers around their neck and curly tufts on their crown.

SIZE:	Male 29 cm; female 23 cm
WHERE TO SEE:	Muddy fields and marshes; sometimes the coast
WHEN TO SEE:	January–December
WHAT THEY EAT:	Mainly worms, insects and their larvae
SOUNDS LIKE:	Mostly silent, but occasionally a low *wek*
LOOKS LIKE:	Redshank

SNIPE

Snipes have round bodies and their feathers are a pattern of brown stripes and bars. Their bills are angled down and very long.

SIZE:	27 cm
WHERE TO SEE:	Around bogs and marshes; more common in winter
WHEN TO SEE:	January–December
WHAT THEY EAT:	Worms and insect larvae
SOUNDS LIKE:	Sharp *scaap* when flushed and a musical *chippa-chippa-chippa*
LOOKS LIKE:	Green sandpiper

BLACK-HEADED GULL

summer

winter

Black-headed gulls are small with a red bill and legs. In summer, they have a dark brown head. They have white underparts with a pale grey back.

SIZE:	37 cm
WHERE TO SEE:	Coastal areas, lakes and marshes
WHEN TO SEE:	January–December
WHAT THEY EAT:	Insects in flight
SOUNDS LIKE:	Harsh *keyaaar* call – their colonies are very noisy!
LOOKS LIKE:	Common gull

KITTIWAKE

Kittiwakes are medium-sized gulls with dark eyes and a small yellow bill. They have grey backs and are white underneath with neat black wing tips and short black legs.

SIZE:	39 cm
WHERE TO SEE:	Sea cliffs
WHEN TO SEE:	January–December
WHAT THEY EAT:	Fish
SOUNDS LIKE:	Mostly silent, but a *kitti-veeek* call by their nest (like their name!)
LOOKS LIKE:	Herring gull, black-headed gull, fulmar

HERRING GULL

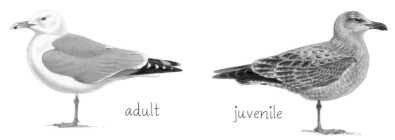

adult   juvenile

SEABIRDS

Herring gulls are large with a white head and underparts, a light grey back and black wing tips. Their legs are pink and their yellow bills are slightly hooked and marked with a red spot. Young herring gulls are brown all over.

SIZE:	56 cm
WHERE TO SEE:	All around the coast
WHEN TO SEE:	January–December
WHAT THEY EAT:	Fish, insects, small animals and carrion
SOUNDS LIKE:	Very noisy – loud mewing and wailing cries, yelps and barks
LOOKS LIKE:	Lesser black-backed gull

LESSER BLACK-BACKED GULL

The lesser black-backed gull is slightly smaller than a herring gull, with yellow legs and dark grey wings and back. Juveniles are similar to young herring gulls, but are darker brown.

SIZE:	53 cm
WHERE TO SEE:	Around the coast, rubbish dumps and ploughed fields
WHEN TO SEE:	January–December (but much more common in summer)
WHAT THEY EAT:	Fish, worms, small birds and scraps
SOUNDS LIKE:	Deep, throaty wailing *ouk ouk* calls
LOOKS LIKE:	Herring gull

GREAT BLACK-BACKED GULL

adult   juvenile

Great black-backed gulls are very large and they have a powerful yellow bill and pinkish legs. They have black backs and a white underside.

SIZE:	66 cm
WHERE TO SEE:	Rocky coasts, large lakes, rubbish dumps and ploughed fields
WHEN TO SEE:	January–December
WHAT THEY EAT:	Small birds, shellfish and carrion
SOUNDS LIKE:	Deep *uk-uk-uk* bark
LOOKS LIKE:	Lesser black-backed gull, herring gull, heron (in flight)

COMMON GULL

Common gulls look like a smaller version of the herring gull. They have greenish legs and a yellow bill and their grey wings have black tips and large white spots.

SIZE:	41 cm
WHERE TO SEE:	Coasts and sometimes playing fields
WHEN TO SEE:	January–December
WHAT THEY EAT:	Worms, insects, fish, carrion and scraps
SOUNDS LIKE:	A shrill *keeee-yaa*
LOOKS LIKE:	Herring gull, young kittiwake

COMMON TERN

Common terns are smaller than gulls, but they do look similar. They are mainly white with silvery-grey upperparts and a black cap on their head. They have a long tail, red legs and a pointed red bill with a black tip.

SIZE:	33 cm
WHERE TO SEE:	Beaches and freshwater areas
WHEN TO SEE:	March–October
WHAT THEY EAT:	Fish and insects
SOUNDS LIKE:	High-pitched *keee-yarrr*
LOOKS LIKE:	Arctic tern, black-headed gull

ARCTIC TERN

Arctic terns migrate further than any other bird. A bird that lives for 25 years may cover more than one million kilometres in its lifetime!

Arctic terns look like the common tern, but their bills are red all over. They are sometimes called 'sea swallows' because of their long, pointed tail streamers.

SIZE:	34 cm
WHERE TO SEE:	Coastal areas, but they spend time at sea
WHEN TO SEE:	March–October
WHAT THEY EAT:	Fish and insects
SOUNDS LIKE:	Sounds like common tern, but higher-pitched
LOOKS LIKE:	Common tern, black-headed gull

LITTLE TERN

Little terns are the smallest of the terns and you can identify them by their sharp yellow bill with a black tip. They also have a white forehead and a black stripe through each eye.

Little terns make their nests right at the edge of the sea. They sometimes even lose their eggs and chicks when the tide comes in!

SIZE:	23 cm
WHERE TO SEE:	Sand and shingle beaches
WHEN TO SEE:	April–October
WHAT THEY EAT:	Fish
SOUNDS LIKE:	Rapid and shrill *krik-krik*
LOOKS LIKE:	Sandwich tern, common tern, Arctic tern

SANDWICH TERN

Of all the terns, Sandwich terns are the largest. They are mostly white, but they have a silvery-grey back and a black cap which is spiky in spring. They have short black legs and a long black bill with a yellow tip.

SIZE:	39 cm
WHERE TO SEE:	Sandy coasts and islands
WHEN TO SEE:	March–October
WHAT THEY EAT:	Fish, especially sand eels
SOUNDS LIKE:	Noisy, harsh *ki-rrick*
LOOKS LIKE:	Common tern, Arctic tern, small gulls

GUILLEMOT

Guillemots look a bit like penguins with their upright posture. They are dark brown with white underparts and a white face and throat in winter. They have a slender, pointed bill and a thin neck.

summer

SIZE:	42 cm
WHERE TO SEE:	Steep sea cliffs
WHEN TO SEE:	January–December
WHAT THEY EAT:	Fish
SOUNDS LIKE:	Very noisy at their nest with a growling *arrrr*
LOOKS LIKE:	Razorbill, puffin

RAZORBILL

Razorbills are the same shape and size as a guillemot, but they are black rather than brown. They also have a larger head, a thicker bill and fine white lines on their bill.

SIZE:	41 cm
WHERE TO SEE:	Steep sea cliffs
WHEN TO SEE:	January–December
WHAT THEY EAT:	Fish
SOUNDS LIKE:	Growling and grunting *caarr* calls at their nest
LOOKS LIKE:	Guillemot, puffin

PUFFIN

Puffins have a brightly coloured flattened bill and large pale cheeks. They are mainly black, with white underparts, orange legs and red and black eye markings.

SIZE:	30 cm
WHERE TO SEE:	Rocky coasts
WHEN TO SEE:	March–November
WHAT THEY EAT:	Fish, especially sand eels
SOUNDS LIKE:	A low growling *arrrr*
LOOKS LIKE:	Razorbill, guillemot

FULMAR

Fulmars look like gulls, but they have nostrils that are like tubes on top of their bill. Their wings are grey and straight.

SIZE:	47 cm
WHERE TO SEE:	All around the coast and far out to sea
WHEN TO SEE:	January–December
WHAT THEY EAT:	Fish waste from boats
SOUNDS LIKE:	Loud, throaty cackling and grunting
LOOKS LIKE:	Herring gull

MANX SHEARWATER

Manx shearwaters are mainly black above, but sometimes look brown in the sun. They have a white throat and underparts and a thin bill.

SIZE:	36 cm
WHERE TO SEE:	All around the coast
WHEN TO SEE:	March–October
WHAT THEY EAT:	Fish, especially herring
SOUNDS LIKE:	Loud wailing noises at nesting sites; *kuk-kuk-kuk-oo* in flight
LOOKS LIKE:	Razorbill

FERAL PIGEON

Feral pigeons come in all shades – blue-grey, greyish-black, reddish-brown – and they often have metallic purple or green on their neck. They usually have a white rump and black wing bars.

SIZE:	32 cm
WHERE TO SEE:	Anywhere from coastal cliffs to city centres
WHEN TO SEE:	January–December
WHAT THEY EAT:	Seeds, berries and cereal from the ground
SOUNDS LIKE:	Cooing calls, *ooo-roo-coo*
LOOKS LIKE:	Collared dove, stock dove, wood pigeon

WOOD PIGEON

Wood pigeons are larger than feral pigeons. They are mainly blue-grey with a pink breast and a greenish-purple neck with a white patch. They have white markings on their wings which you can see in flight.

SIZE:	41 cm
WHERE TO SEE:	Woods, parks, gardens and farmland
WHEN TO SEE:	January–December
WHAT THEY EAT:	Fruit, nuts, berries, seeds and crops like cabbages, peas and grain
SOUNDS LIKE:	Rhythmic five-part cooing, *coo-ROO-roo, oo-roo*
LOOKS LIKE:	Collared dove, stock dove, feral pigeon

STOCK DOVE

Stock doves look very similar to feral pigeons. They have a blue-grey body, a greenish neck and black bars on their wings.

SIZE:	33 cm
WHERE TO SEE:	Parks and woodlands
WHEN TO SEE:	January–December
WHAT THEY EAT:	Seeds
SOUNDS LIKE:	Rhythmic two-part cooing, *ooo-woo, ooo-woo*
LOOKS LIKE:	Feral pigeon, wood pigeon

TURTLE DOVE

Turtle doves have orange-brown backs with a black spot pattern and a black tail. They have a black and white striped neck patch.

SIZE:	28 cm
WHERE TO SEE:	Woodlands, farmland, hedgerows and bushes
WHEN TO SEE:	April–September, but very rare
WHAT THEY EAT:	Seeds and weeds
SOUNDS LIKE:	Cat-like purring, *rooorrr rooorrr*
LOOKS LIKE:	Collared dove, feral pigeon

COLLARED DOVE

Collared doves are larger than turtle doves and less colourful. They are pinky-brown and have a black marking around their neck.

SIZE:	30 cm
WHERE TO SEE:	Gardens and parks
WHEN TO SEE:	January–December
WHAT THEY EAT:	Seeds and grain
SOUNDS LIKE:	Rhythmic three-part cooing, *coo–COO-coo*
LOOKS LIKE:	Turtle dove, wood pigeon, feral pigeon

BARN OWL

Barn owls have pure white underparts and a heart-shaped face with large dark eyes. Their back and wings are golden-brown with grey spots.

SIZE:	34 cm
WHERE TO SEE:	Woodlands and farmland; close to riverbanks
WHEN TO SEE:	January–December; nocturnal
WHAT THEY EAT:	Field mice, voles and shrews
SOUNDS LIKE:	Eerie shrieks – sometimes they are known as 'screech owls'
LOOKS LIKE:	Tawny owl, short-eared owl

TAWNY OWL

Tawny owls are the same size as a pigeon, with a big, round head and black eyes. Their plumage is grey and brown with white dappled markings on their head, back and wings.

SIZE:	38 cm
WHERE TO SEE:	Woodlands, farms and parks
WHEN TO SEE:	January–December; nocturnal
WHAT THEY EAT:	Small mammals, birds and frogs
SOUNDS LIKE:	Long three-part *hoo-hoo-hoo*; females call *ker-wick*
LOOKS LIKE:	Barn owl, long-eared owl, short-eared owl

LITTLE OWL

Little owls are the same size as a starling and their large yellow eyes have fierce-looking eyebrows.

SIZE:	34 cm
WHERE TO SEE:	Farmland and parkland with plenty of trees
WHEN TO SEE:	January–December; nocturnal
WHAT THEY EAT:	Large insects, small rodents and birds
SOUNDS LIKE:	Musical, rising *kiew kiew kiew*
LOOKS LIKE:	Tawny owl, short-eared owl

SHORT-EARED OWL

Short-eared owls have small feathered 'ears' which are hard to see. They have fierce yellow eyes and a border around their face.

SIZE:	37 cm
WHERE TO SEE:	Marshland, moorland and meadows
WHEN TO SEE:	January–December; nocturnal
WHAT THEY EAT:	Small rodents, especially voles, and small birds
SOUNDS LIKE:	Deep *boo-boo-boo*, but usually silent
LOOKS LIKE:	Tawny owl, long-eared owl, barn owl

LONG-EARED OWL

Long-eared owls have long tufts which look like feathered 'ears'. Their plumage is a mixture of browns and black and they have deep orange eyes.

SIZE:	34 cm
WHERE TO SEE:	Woodlands and forests
WHEN TO SEE:	January–December; nocturnal
WHAT THEY EAT:	Small rodents, especially field mice, and small birds
SOUNDS LIKE:	Low, moaning *ooo-ooo-ooo*
LOOKS LIKE:	Short-eared owl, tawny owl, barn owl

GREEN WOODPECKER

Woodpeckers hop up trees by jerkily clinging on with their feet. They drum their bills against tree trunks, making a hammering noise.

Green woodpeckers have bright red caps, pale green cheeks and a bright green back. They have black face markings and a dark red moustache.

SIZE:	32 cm
WHERE TO SEE:	Woodlands and parks
WHEN TO SEE:	January–December
WHAT THEY EAT:	Ants – they use their tongue to take ants from their nests
SOUNDS LIKE:	Loud laughing *gluck-gluck-gluck*
LOOKS LIKE:	Great spotted woodpecker

GREAT SPOTTED WOODPECKER

Great spotted woodpeckers have bold black and white plumage and a pointed bill and tail. They have a bright red patch on the back of their head and underneath their tail. They spend most of their time clinging to the side of tree trunks with their tail pressed against the bark.

SIZE:	23 cm
WHERE TO SEE:	Woodlands and parks
WHEN TO SEE:	January–December
WHAT THEY EAT:	Insects, seeds and berries
SOUNDS LIKE:	Loud *tchick-tchick* call
LOOKS LIKE:	Green woodpecker

KINGFISHER

Kingfishers are small, stocky birds with bright blue and orange plumage. They have tiny red legs and a large, pointed black bill.

SIZE:	17 cm
WHERE TO SEE:	Streams, rivers and lakes
WHEN TO SEE:	January–December
WHAT THEY EAT:	Small fish, tadpoles and water insects
SOUNDS LIKE:	Sharp, shrill *cheee*

NIGHTJAR

Nightjars have a long tail and long wings with white markings. They have a mottled and spotted grey-brown body and large black eyes. They are nocturnal.

SIZE:	27 cm
WHERE TO SEE:	Mainly heathland and woodland clearings
WHEN TO SEE:	April–September
WHAT THEY EAT:	Insects and moths
SOUNDS LIKE:	Vibrant *cooo-ick* in flight; also a purring song sometimes for up to 5 minutes without a break

CUCKOO

Cuckoos are dove-sized and (with their pointed wings and tail) they look a bit like a bird of prey.

SIZE:	30 cm
WHERE TO SEE:	Mainly moorland
WHEN TO SEE:	April–September
WHAT THEY EAT:	Insects, especially caterpillars
SOUNDS LIKE:	Loud *cuc-koo* in spring; also laughing *kow-kow-kow* if alarmed
LOOKS LIKE:	Kestrel, sparrowhawk, pigeons

SWIFT

Swifts are larger than swallows and they have long, curved wings and a short, forked tail. They are blackish-brown with a white throat.

Swifts are superb flyers – they can even sleep in the air! They sometimes spend three years in flight without landing once!

SIZE:	17 cm
WHERE TO SEE:	Villages and towns, especially near lakes
WHEN TO SEE:	April–September
WHAT THEY EAT:	Flying insects
SOUNDS LIKE:	Loud screaming *screeee*, often in groups
LOOKS LIKE:	Swallow

SWALLOW

Swallows have very long tail streamers and narrow, pointed wings. Their plumage is metallic dark blue with creamy-white underparts and a red chin.

SIZE:	19 cm
WHERE TO SEE:	Rivers, streams and farmland with ponds
WHEN TO SEE:	March–October
WHAT THEY EAT:	Flying insects, mostly large flies
SOUNDS LIKE:	Light *tswit-tswit* call; long twittering song
LOOKS LIKE:	Swift, house martin

HOUSE MARTIN

House martins are slightly smaller than swallows and they also have a forked tail, but with no tail streamers. Their upper body is metallic blue and black and they have a white rump.

SIZE:	13 cm
WHERE TO SEE:	Villages and farmland
WHEN TO SEE:	March–October
WHAT THEY EAT:	Small flying insects and spiders
SOUNDS LIKE:	*Chirrup* call; soft twittering song
LOOKS LIKE:	Swallow, swift

SAND MARTIN

Sand martins are slimmer than house martins. They have brown upperparts with white underneath and a brown band across their breast.

SIZE:	12 cm
WHERE TO SEE:	Open countryside, usually near water, and sandy coastal cliffs
WHEN TO SEE:	April–October
WHAT THEY EAT:	Small flying insects
SOUNDS LIKE:	Low *chirrup* call; soft twittering song
LOOKS LIKE:	Swallow, swift

DUNNOCK

Dunnocks are the same size as a sparrow, but slightly slimmer and with a thinner bill. They are mainly brown with black streaks and a grey head and breast.

SIZE:	14 cm
WHERE TO SEE:	Woodlands, parks and gardens
WHEN TO SEE:	January–December
WHAT THEY EAT:	Small insects, spiders and seeds
SOUNDS LIKE:	Loud, high *tseep* call; fast warbling song
LOOKS LIKE:	Sparrow, robin, wren

SKYLARK

Skylarks are slightly larger than a sparrow and their upperparts are streaked brown. They have white underparts and outer tail feathers and a short crest on their head.

SIZE:	18 cm
WHERE TO SEE:	Open countryside
WHEN TO SEE:	January–December
WHAT THEY EAT:	Seeds, plants, insects and spiders
SOUNDS LIKE:	Loud *chirrup* call; warbling song
LOOKS LIKE:	Meadow pipit, reed bunting

MEADOW PIPIT

Meadow pipits are smaller than a skylark with a thinner bill and no crest. They are streaky brown and cream underneath, with pale orange legs.

SIZE:	14 cm
WHERE TO SEE:	Damp meadows, moorland and sand dunes
WHEN TO SEE:	January–December
WHAT THEY EAT:	Insects and seeds
SOUNDS LIKE:	Weak *peep-peep-peep* call; high-pitched song
LOOKS LIKE:	Rock pipit

ROCK PIPIT

Rock pipits are larger than meadow pipits and they have dark brown, heavily streaked plumage. They have a dark bill and legs.

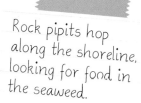

Rock pipits hop along the shoreline, looking for food in the seaweed.

SIZE:	17 cm
WHERE TO SEE:	At the base of cliffs and along the shoreline
WHEN TO SEE:	January–December
WHAT THEY EAT:	Insects
SOUNDS LIKE:	Whistling *pseep* call; song like meadow pipit but fuller
LOOKS LIKE:	Meadow pipit, skylark

SONGBIRDS

PIED WAGTAIL

Pied wagtails are sparrow-sized with a long tail. Males are mainly black with white markings. Females have more grey feathers.

male

SIZE:	18 cm
WHERE TO SEE:	Countryside and gardens; often in towns
WHEN TO SEE:	January–December
WHAT THEY EAT:	Insects and seeds
SOUNDS LIKE:	Sharp *tissik* flight call; simple warbling song
LOOKS LIKE:	Grey wagtail, yellow wagtail

YELLOW WAGTAIL

Yellow wagtails are small birds, with medium-length tails and thin black legs.

SIZE:	17 cm
WHERE TO SEE:	Farmland and marshes
WHEN TO SEE:	April–October
WHAT THEY EAT:	Insects
SOUNDS LIKE:	Loud *twseep* call; simple warbling song
LOOKS LIKE:	Pied wagtail, grey wagtail

GREY WAGTAIL

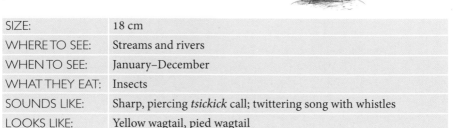

Grey wagtails are a similar size to pied wagtails, but with a longer tail. Males have a yellow chest and black throat in summer.

female

SIZE:	18 cm
WHERE TO SEE:	Streams and rivers
WHEN TO SEE:	January–December
WHAT THEY EAT:	Insects
SOUNDS LIKE:	Sharp, piercing *tsickick* call; twittering song with whistles
LOOKS LIKE:	Yellow wagtail, pied wagtail

DIPPER

Dippers are plump blackish-brown birds with a white chest and a brown band on their belly.

SIZE:	18 cm
WHERE TO SEE:	Fast-flowing streams
WHEN TO SEE:	January–December
WHAT THEY EAT:	Water insects and their eggs
SOUNDS LIKE:	Sharp *zit zit* call; soft warbling song
LOOKS LIKE:	Wren

WAXWING

Waxwings are reddish-brown birds with a black throat and a line through each eye. They have a large crest and their wings and tail have yellow and white feathers.

SIZE:	17 cm
WHERE TO SEE:	Gardens – anywhere where there are plants with berries
WHEN TO SEE:	November–April; some years they visit in very large numbers
WHAT THEY EAT:	Insects, berries and fruit
SOUNDS LIKE:	High *sirrrrrrr*
LOOKS LIKE:	Starling

WREN

Wrens are tiny with a short, upright tail. They are reddish-brown with faint black stripes, pale underparts and a pale stripe above each eye.

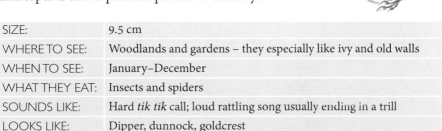

SIZE:	9.5 cm
WHERE TO SEE:	Woodlands and gardens – they especially like ivy and old walls
WHEN TO SEE:	January–December
WHAT THEY EAT:	Insects and spiders
SOUNDS LIKE:	Hard *tik tik* call; loud rattling song usually ending in a trill
LOOKS LIKE:	Dipper, dunnock, goldcrest

SONGBIRDS

STONECHAT

Stonechats are about the size of a robin and they also have an orange-red breast. Males have a black tail and head with white around the side of their neck. Females are mainly brown, but also have an orange tinge to their chests.

male

female

SIZE:	13 cm
WHERE TO SEE:	Moorland and coastland with heather
WHEN TO SEE:	January–December
WHAT THEY EAT:	Insects, seeds and fruit
SOUNDS LIKE:	*Wee-tak tak* call, like stones struck together; short, quivering song
LOOKS LIKE:	Wheatear, redstart, robin

WHEATEAR

Wheatears are larger than robins. They are blue-grey above with black wings and a black patch through their eye. They have a light orange breast and a white rump.

male

female

SIZE:	15 cm
WHERE TO SEE:	Mountains and rocky moorland
WHEN TO SEE:	March–October
WHAT THEY EAT:	Insects and spiders
SOUNDS LIKE:	*Wee-tak tak* call like a stonechat; warbling song
LOOKS LIKE:	Stonechat

ROBIN

Robins are the same size as sparrows with a big head and a small, thin bill. These plump brown birds have a bright orange-red throat and a white belly.

Robins are often known as 'gardeners' friends' because they perch nearby when soil is being turned over and quickly feed on any insects.

SIZE:	14 cm
WHERE TO SEE:	Gardens, hedgerows and woodlands
WHEN TO SEE:	January–December
WHAT THEY EAT:	Worms, seeds, fruit and insects
SOUNDS LIKE:	Rapid *tic tic* call; warbling, melancholy song – sometimes at night
LOOKS LIKE:	Dunnock, redstart, nightingale, black redstart

REDSTART

Male redstarts have a black throat and face with a white forehead. They are blue-grey above and orange-red below with a bright red tail. Females are more brown, but still with a bright tail.

female

male

SIZE:	14 cm
WHERE TO SEE:	Woodlands, gardens and parks
WHEN TO SEE:	March–October
WHAT THEY EAT:	Insects, spiders, worms and berries
SOUNDS LIKE:	*Wheeet* note like a willow warbler; hurried jingle song
LOOKS LIKE:	Robin

SPOTTED FLYCATCHER

Spotted flycatchers are mainly grey-brown and pale underneath with a streaky breast and forehead. Their eyes, legs and bill are black.

Spotted flycatchers dart out from their perch to grab insects, then return to the same spot.

SIZE:	14 cm
WHERE TO SEE:	Woodlands, parks and gardens
WHEN TO SEE:	May–October
WHAT THEY EAT:	Flying insects
SOUNDS LIKE:	Short, unmusical *zeee* call; scratchy, weak song
LOOKS LIKE:	Young robin, redstart, pied flycatcher

PIED FLYCATCHER

Male pied flycatchers are mostly black and white with a bold white patch on their wing. Females are a dull brown, also with white wing patches.

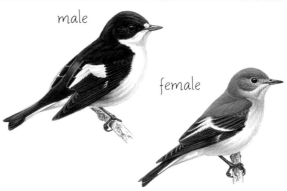

male

female

SIZE:	13 cm
WHERE TO SEE:	Wooded hillsides
WHEN TO SEE:	April–October
WHAT THEY EAT:	Insects
SOUNDS LIKE:	Sharp *huit* call; short, simple *tzit tzit trui trui* song
LOOKS LIKE:	Spotted flycatcher

BLACKBIRD

Male blackbirds are as you'd expect – black all over except for a yellow bill and ring around the eye. Females are actually dark brown with a paler throat and breast.

male

female

SIZE:	25 cm
WHERE TO SEE:	Woodlands, gardens and parks
WHEN TO SEE:	January–December
WHAT THEY EAT:	Insects, worms and berries
SOUNDS LIKE:	Low *tchook-tchook* call; rich, flute-like, melodic song
LOOKS LIKE:	Song thrush

FIELDFARE

Fieldfares have a brown back and blue-grey head. Their breast is speckled brown and they have a short, thin yellow bill and dark tail. Fieldfares usually fly, feed and roost together in flocks.

SIZE:	25 cm
WHERE TO SEE:	Parks, fields and orchards
WHEN TO SEE:	October–April
WHAT THEY EAT:	Insects, worms, snails and berries
SOUNDS LIKE:	Loud *chak-chak-chak* call; song is various squeaks and whistles
LOOKS LIKE:	Female blackbird, mistle thrush

SONGBIRDS

SONG THRUSH

Song thrushes have brown backs and a speckled cream breast. They are slightly smaller than a blackbird.

SIZE:	23 cm
WHERE TO SEE:	Woodlands, gardens and fields
WHEN TO SEE:	January–December
WHAT THEY EAT:	Mainly snails, but also worms, berries and insects
SOUNDS LIKE:	Soft *tsip* call; loud, tuneful song with repeated phrases
LOOKS LIKE:	Female blackbird, mistle thrush, redwing, fieldfare, starling

REDWING

Redwings have brown plumage with pale, spotted underparts. They have red flanks and a bold white eye-stripe.

SIZE:	21 cm
WHERE TO SEE:	Woodlands and fields
WHEN TO SEE:	September–April
WHAT THEY EAT:	Berries and worms
SOUNDS LIKE:	Soft *seeep* call; falling whistling song
LOOKS LIKE:	Song thrush, mistle thrush, fieldfare, starling, female blackbird

MISTLE THRUSH

Mistle thrushes are one of the largest types of thrush, with a grey-brown back and a white breast covered with black spots.

SIZE:	27 cm
WHERE TO SEE:	Woodlands, gardens and parks
WHEN TO SEE:	January–December
WHAT THEY EAT:	Berries and worms
SOUNDS LIKE:	Loud rattling *tsarrk*; flute-like song like a blackbird
LOOKS LIKE:	Song thrush, fieldfare, female blackbird, green woodpecker

STARLING

Starlings are black with a metallic green and purple shine. In the winter they have small pale flecks over their body and wings.

winter

SIZE:	22 cm
WHERE TO SEE:	Woodlands, gardens and parks
WHEN TO SEE:	January–December
WHAT THEY EAT:	Insects, worms and seeds
SOUNDS LIKE:	Complicated song with rattles, gurgles and whistles
LOOKS LIKE:	Blackbird, jackdaw, waxwing

SEDGE WARBLER

Sedge warblers are small, plump birds with a striking white stripe above each eye. They are streaky brown above and paler below.

SIZE:	13 cm
WHERE TO SEE:	Wetlands with scrub and bushes
WHEN TO SEE:	April–September
WHAT THEY EAT:	Insects and spiders
SOUNDS LIKE:	Dry *chirr chirr* call; chattering song with sweet notes and chirrups
LOOKS LIKE:	Reed warbler, wren

REED WARBLER

Reed warblers are plain brown birds with pale eyebrows. They have a longer bill than the sedge warbler and a white throat.

SIZE:	13 cm
WHERE TO SEE:	Reed beds and plants close to water
WHEN TO SEE:	April–October
WHAT THEY EAT:	Insects and spiders
SOUNDS LIKE:	Sharp *chrrr* call; chattering song – less lively than a sedge warbler's
LOOKS LIKE:	Sedge warbler

BLACKCAP

Blackcaps are stocky greyish-brown birds. The male birds have a small black cap.

male

female

SIZE:	14 cm
WHERE TO SEE:	Woodlands, gardens and parks
WHEN TO SEE:	January–December
WHAT THEY EAT:	Insects and berries
SOUNDS LIKE:	Harsh *tak* call; loud warbling song
LOOKS LIKE:	Whitethroat, marsh tit

WHITETHROAT

Male whitethroats have a grey head, a white throat and a brown back. Females are more brown, but they still have the white throat.

female

SIZE:	14 cm
WHERE TO SEE:	Hedgerows and bushes
WHEN TO SEE:	April–October
WHAT THEY EAT:	Insects, berries and fruit
SOUNDS LIKE:	Harsh *tak tak* call; short, scratchy song
LOOKS LIKE:	Blackcap

WILLOW WARBLER

Willow warblers are very small and neat with olive-green plumage, long wing tips and a yellow eye-stripe.

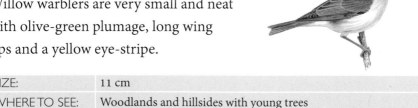

SIZE:	11 cm
WHERE TO SEE:	Woodlands and hillsides with young trees
WHEN TO SEE:	April–September
WHAT THEY EAT:	Small insects, spiders, berries and fruit
SOUNDS LIKE:	Soft, repeated *hoo-eet* call; soft song ending with a flourish
LOOKS LIKE:	Chiffchaff, wood warbler

CHIFFCHAFF

Chiffchaffs look just like a willow warbler,
except they are browner, with darker legs
and short wing tips.

SIZE:	11 cm
WHERE TO SEE:	Woodlands, gardens and parks
WHEN TO SEE:	January–December
WHAT THEY EAT:	Insects
SOUNDS LIKE:	*Hweet* call; repetitive *chiff-chaff chiff-chaff* song
LOOKS LIKE:	Willow warbler, wood warbler

WOOD WARBLER

Wood warblers are larger than other warblers
with a shorter tail. They have greenish
upperparts, a yellow throat and a white belly.

SIZE:	13 cm
WHERE TO SEE:	Wooded hillsides with old trees
WHEN TO SEE:	April–September
WHAT THEY EAT:	Insects and spiders
SOUNDS LIKE:	Loud *sweet* call; low *sioo sioo sioo* or fast *ti-ti-ti-ti-ikirrrrr* song
LOOKS LIKE:	Willow warbler, chiffchaff

WHINCHAT

Whinchats have a bold white stripe above
each eye. They are streaky brown above and
orange-buff underneath.

SIZE:	13 cm
WHERE TO SEE:	Meadows, moorland and open countryside with bracken beds
WHEN TO SEE:	April–September
WHAT THEY EAT:	Insects
SOUNDS LIKE:	Hard *tic-tic tu-tic tic* call; robin-like song
LOOKS LIKE:	Wheatear, sedge warbler

SONGBIRDS

GOLDCREST

Goldcrests are Britain's smallest bird. They are round and greyish-green and they have an orange crest with a black stripe on each side.

SIZE:	9 cm
WHERE TO SEE:	Woodlands and parks, especially with conifer trees
WHEN TO SEE:	January–December
WHAT THEY EAT:	Insects and spiders
SOUNDS LIKE:	High-pitched *zee-zee* call; high-pitched song
LOOKS LIKE:	Firecrest, willow warbler, chiffchaff, wren

NUTHATCH

Nuthatches are plump birds that look a bit like a small woodpecker. They have a bold black stripe through their eye, a big head and a black, pointed bill.

SIZE:	14 cm
WHERE TO SEE:	Woodlands, gardens and parks
WHEN TO SEE:	January–December
WHAT THEY EAT:	Insects and seeds
SOUNDS LIKE:	Loud piping *tuit tuituit* call; whistling song
LOOKS LIKE:	Blue tit, great tit, treecreeper, woodpeckers

TREECREEPER

Treecreepers are small birds with a pointed tail and a thin, downcurved bill. They have a white belly and eyebrow marking.

SIZE:	13 cm
WHERE TO SEE:	Woodlands
WHEN TO SEE:	January–December
WHAT THEY EAT:	Insects
SOUNDS LIKE:	High-pitched *tsit* call; song is a falling series of notes
LOOKS LIKE:	Nuthatch, wren

LONG-TAILED TIT

Long-tailed tits are tiny birds with a very long tail. They have a pink and black back, and are pinkish and fluffy below. They have bold black eyebrow markings, too.

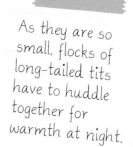

As they are so small, flocks of long-tailed tits have to huddle together for warmth at night.

SIZE:	14 cm
WHERE TO SEE:	Woodlands, gardens and parks
WHEN TO SEE:	January–December
WHAT THEY EAT:	Insects and spiders
SOUNDS LIKE:	High-pitched *zee-zee* call with hissing *trrrr* trills
LOOKS LIKE:	Pied wagtail, coal tit

COAL TIT

Coal tits are the smallest of the tit family and have a grey back, a black cap and white markings on their cheeks, wings and on the back of their neck.

SIZE:	11 cm
WHERE TO SEE:	Woodlands and parks with conifers
WHEN TO SEE:	January–December
WHAT THEY EAT:	Insects and seeds
SOUNDS LIKE:	High *tsee* call; bright two-part *see-too, see-too* song
LOOKS LIKE:	Great tit, marsh tit

BLUE TIT

Blue tits are small, lively birds with a blue head, tail and wings. They have a yellow breast, white cheeks and a black eye-stripe.

SIZE:	11 cm
WHERE TO SEE:	Woodlands, gardens and parks
WHEN TO SEE:	January–December
WHAT THEY EAT:	Insects and seeds
SOUNDS LIKE:	Thin, rising *see see* call; high trilling song
LOOKS LIKE:	Great tit, marsh tit

GREAT TIT

Bird tables are a great place to see all types of tits, often fighting over the food.

Great tits are sparrow-sized and the largest of all the British tits. They have a green back, blue wings and tail and a bright yellow chest. Their head is glossy black with white cheeks.

SIZE:	14 cm
WHERE TO SEE:	Woodlands, gardens and parks
WHEN TO SEE:	January–December
WHAT THEY EAT:	Insects, berries and seeds
SOUNDS LIKE:	*Chink* call; lots of different songs, including *tea-cher tea-cher*
LOOKS LIKE:	Blue tit, coal tit

Marsh tits are small, mainly brown birds with a shiny black cap, a small black bib and a pale belly.

SIZE:	12 cm
WHERE TO SEE:	Woodlands and parks – not marshes!
WHEN TO SEE:	January–December
WHAT THEY EAT:	Insects and seeds
SOUNDS LIKE:	Shrill *pitchu* call; repeated *chip chip chip* song
LOOKS LIKE:	Coal tit, blackcap

JAY

Jays are pinky-brown, pigeon-sized birds with black and white wings with a bright blue patch. They have a streaked, pale crest on their forehead and a white rump in flight.

SONGBIRDS

SIZE:	32 cm
WHERE TO SEE:	Woodlands, parks and gardens
WHEN TO SEE:	January–December
WHAT THEY EAT:	Acorns, nuts, seeds and insects, but also nestlings of other birds
SOUNDS LIKE:	Loud *skark skark* and loud screech
LOOKS LIKE:	Magpie

MAGPIE

In spring, magpies often come together in large flocks called 'murders'. They sometimes even attack cats and other birds!

Magpies are large black and white birds with very long tails. Sometimes their black parts shine green or blue.

SIZE:	46 cm
WHERE TO SEE:	Farmland, gardens and parks
WHEN TO SEE:	January–December
WHAT THEY EAT:	Worms, snails, insects and nestlings
SOUNDS LIKE:	Loud and harsh *chacka-chacka-chacka*
LOOKS LIKE:	Jay

CARRION CROW

Crows are larger than magpies, and black all over with a bluish-purple shine. They have a short, heavy, powerful bill and strong claws.

Hooded crows are very similar to carrion crows, but they have a pale grey back and belly.

SIZE:	47 cm
WHERE TO SEE:	Farmland, woodlands, parks, villages, towns and coasts
WHEN TO SEE:	January–December
WHAT THEY EAT:	Carrion, nestlings, insects, worms, seeds, fruit and scraps
SOUNDS LIKE:	Loud, deep *kraa-kraa*
LOOKS LIKE:	Rook, raven, jackdaw

RAVEN

Ravens are the largest and most powerful of the crow family. They are all black with a massive bill, shaggy feathers on their throat and long wings.

SIZE:	64 cm
WHERE TO SEE:	Woodlands, mountains and rocky coasts
WHEN TO SEE:	January–December
WHAT THEY EAT:	Carrion, insects, worms, seeds, fruit and scraps
SOUNDS LIKE:	Deep *kronk kronk* croak
LOOKS LIKE:	Rook, carrion crow, hooded crow, large birds of prey

ROOK

Rooks look a lot like carrion crows, but you can tell them apart because rooks have shaggier leg feathers and a bare grey patch at the base of their bill.

Although not known for their song, rooks and crows are a member of the songbird, or perching bird, family. Songbirds include almost half the world's birds!

SIZE:	46 cm
WHERE TO SEE:	Woodlands and farmland
WHEN TO SEE:	January–December
WHAT THEY EAT:	Worms, grain, mice and insects
SOUNDS LIKE:	Very loud *cawww*
LOOKS LIKE:	Carrion crow, hooded crow, raven, jackdaw

JACKDAW

Jackdaws are smaller than rooks and have neat, upright bodies. They have black, glossy plumage with paler feathers on their neck and a white eye-ring.

SIZE:	33 cm
WHERE TO SEE:	Woodlands, parks and old ruins
WHEN TO SEE:	January–December
WHAT THEY EAT:	Insects, nestlings, worms, berries, seeds and scraps
SOUNDS LIKE:	Short, sharp *jack jack*, and high-pitched *kyow*
LOOKS LIKE:	Carrion crow, hooded crow, rook, feral pigeon

CROSSBILL

male

female

Crossbills use their bill to prise open pine cones and eat the seeds from inside.

Crossbills are chunky birds and they have a large head. Their bill is crossed at the tip. Females are greenish-brown and males are brick red.

SIZE:	16 cm
WHERE TO SEE:	Woodlands, especially near mountains
WHEN TO SEE:	January–December
WHAT THEY EAT:	Seeds from conifers
SOUNDS LIKE:	Loud *chip-chip-chip* calls

HOUSE SPARROW

House sparrows are small and plump. Males have grey caps and chests, and a black patch on the throat, upper chest and eyebrow. Females are a more dull, streaky brown and paler below.

male

SIZE:	15 cm
WHERE TO SEE:	Towns and villages
WHEN TO SEE:	January–December
WHAT THEY EAT:	Seeds, berries, insects and scraps
SOUNDS LIKE:	Simple chirps and chirrups
LOOKS LIKE:	Tree sparrow, dunnock, chaffinch (female)

TREE SPARROW

Tree sparrows are smaller than house sparrows, and they look very similar. Their heads have a chestnut cap and white faces with black patches on their checks.

SIZE:	14 cm
WHERE TO SEE:	Open countryside, gardens and parks
WHEN TO SEE:	January–December
WHAT THEY EAT:	Insects and seeds
SOUNDS LIKE:	Loud, high-pitched chirruping and cheeping; *tek tek* in flight
LOOKS LIKE:	House sparrow

REED BUNTING

male · female

Reed buntings have a brown, streaky back and paler underparts.
Males have a black head, with a white collar and moustache.

SIZE:	15 cm
WHERE TO SEE:	Riverbanks and marshy areas
WHEN TO SEE:	January–December
WHAT THEY EAT:	Insects and seeds
SOUNDS LIKE:	Loud *tseek* call; song is repeated chirps
LOOKS LIKE:	Yellowhammer, house sparrow, tree sparrow

YELLOWHAMMER

male · female

Male yellowhammers have a bright yellow head and breast. Their backs
are streaked brown and they have a long tail. Females are much less
yellow, with heavier brown streaking.

SIZE:	17 cm
WHERE TO SEE:	Farmland and scrubby areas
WHEN TO SEE:	January–December
WHAT THEY EAT:	Insects and seeds
SOUNDS LIKE:	Grating *zit* call; song with deep final note *se-se-se-se-se-se-se-soo*
LOOKS LIKE:	Reed bunting

CHAFFINCH

male

female

Male chaffinches have rosy pink breasts and cheeks with a grey head. They have white bands on their wings and a brown tail. Females are more pinkish-brown.

SIZE:	15 cm
WHERE TO SEE:	Woodlands, gardens and parks
WHEN TO SEE:	January–December
WHAT THEY EAT:	Insects and seeds
SOUNDS LIKE:	Loud *chink chink* call; bright rattling song ending in a flourish
LOOKS LIKE:	House sparrow (female), brambling

GOLDFINCH

Goldfinches are small sandy-brown birds with red, black and white faces. They have golden bars on their black and brown wings.

SIZE:	12 cm
WHERE TO SEE:	Gardens, parks, orchards and villages
WHEN TO SEE:	January–December
WHAT THEY EAT:	Insects and seeds
SOUNDS LIKE:	Simple *twit-a-twit* call; long twittering song like a swallow
LOOKS LIKE:	Greenfinch, siskin, linnet

SONGBIRDS

GREENFINCH

male

female

Male greenfinches are mostly bright green, whereas females have more brown in their plumage. They both have yellow markings on their wings and tail.

SIZE:	15 cm
WHERE TO SEE:	Woodlands, parks and gardens
WHEN TO SEE:	January–December
WHAT THEY EAT:	Insects and seeds
SOUNDS LIKE:	Loud *chup* call; wheezy song with whistles and twitters
LOOKS LIKE:	Siskin, goldfinch, yellowhammer, house sparrow (female)

SISKIN

female

male

Siskins are smaller than greenfinches. Males have streaky green upperparts with a yellow breast and face and a black crown and chin. Females are streakier and don't have a black face.

SIZE:	11 cm
WHERE TO SEE:	Woodlands and parks
WHEN TO SEE:	January–December
WHAT THEY EAT:	Insects and seeds
SOUNDS LIKE:	Squeaky *tzeuu* call; twittering song
LOOKS LIKE:	Greenfinch, goldfinch

BRAMBLING

Bramblings are similar in size to a chaffinch. They have a bright orange breast and wing bars, a white rump, and males have a black head in spring.

SIZE:	15 cm
WHERE TO SEE:	Woodlands
WHEN TO SEE:	October–April
WHAT THEY EAT:	Insects and seeds
SOUNDS LIKE:	Deep buzzing *dzeeee*
LOOKS LIKE:	Chaffinch, house sparrow

BULLFINCH

male

Bullfinches are plump, shy birds with a thick neck and bill. Males have a grey back, a rosy red breast and a black crown, whereas females are a duller brown.

SIZE:	15 cm
WHERE TO SEE:	Woodlands, gardens and parks
WHEN TO SEE:	January–December
WHAT THEY EAT:	Insects, seeds and berries
SOUNDS LIKE:	Soft *pee-uu* call; quiet, creaky song
LOOKS LIKE:	Chaffinch, robin

LINNET

male

Male linnets have a chestnut back, a grey head and a red forehead and patches on their breast in summer. Females are streaky brown.

SIZE:	13 cm
WHERE TO SEE:	Farmland, gardens and parks
WHEN TO SEE:	January–December
WHAT THEY EAT:	Seeds
SOUNDS LIKE:	*Tsooeet* call; twittering, musical song
LOOKS LIKE:	Chaffinch

SONGBIRDS

93

GLOSSARY

Barred
Marked with stripes of distinctive colour.

Bill
A bird's beak.

Breeding season
The time of year when birds build nests, mate, lay eggs and raise young.

Camouflage
Markings which help an animal to blend in to their surroundings.

Carrion
The rotten flesh of dead animals, often eaten by scavenging birds.

Colony
A group of birds that live close together.

Cover
An area where you can't easily be seen, e.g. behind a bush.

Dabbling
Searching for food just below the surface of the water.

Dawn chorus
Many birds singing together at the start of a spring day.

Drumming
The rhythmic sound made by a woodpecker banging its bill on a tree trunk or a bird beating its wings together in flight.

Flock
A group of birds that live, travel or feed together.

Flush
Causing a bird to fly off, usually by getting too close to it.

Game bird
A bird that is hunted for its meat, such as a pheasant.

Habitat
A particular type of place where a group of animals or plants lives, such as mountains or an estuary.

Identification
Working out the name of a bird.

Juvenile
A young bird, often with different plumage to an adult of the same species.

Larvae
The young of certain animals that must drastically change physically before they become adults, e.g. tadpoles, maggots, caterpillars.

Migrant
Any bird that spends the winter in one place and the summer in another.

Migration
The seasonal movement of a species from one area to another.

Moult
To lose feathers to make way for new ones.

Nestling
A baby bird that has not yet learnt to fly.

Nocturnal
Active at night, as owls are.

Perch
A resting place on which a bird lands or roosts, such as a telegraph pole.

Plumage
All of a bird's feathers.

Predator
An animal that hunts other animals for food.

Prey
An animal hunted by other animals for food.

Reed
A tall grass that grows in shallow water.

Roost
A place where a bird sleeps.

Ruff
A ring of feathers around the neck of a bird.

Scavenger
An animal that feeds on carrion or waste.

Scrub
Land that is covered with small bushes and trees.

Shingle
Small stones on a beach.

Songbird
Any bird with a musical song or call.

Species
A particular kind of animal.

Underparts
The lower half of a bird, including its throat, breast and belly.

Upending
Feeding by tipping upside down, so a bird's head is under the water and its tail is in the air.

Upperparts
The upper half of a bird, including its head, neck, back, wings and rump.

Wader
A bird, such as a sandpiper or plover, that uses its long legs to wade in shallow water in the search for food.

Warbling
Singing with trills and quivering notes.

Webbcd feet
Feet which have a layer of skin stretched between the toes.

Wetland
A habitat which is mainly water, such as a lake.

Wing bar
A stripe of colour across the feathers on a birds wing.

INDEX